To:

_____

From:

_____

Date:

_____

Jesus
Name Above All Names

ROY LESSIN

Pi **Pocket**
INSPIRATIONS

summerside
PRESS

Jesus, Name Above All Names

By Roy Lessin
A *Pocket Inspirations* Book

Copyright © 2011 by Roy Lessin

Published by Summerside Press™
Minneapolis 55438
www.summersidepress.com

Designed by Lisa & Jeff Franke

ISBN 978-1-60936-122-8

Scripture references are from the following sources: The Holy Bible, King James Version (KJV). The New King James Version (NKJV). Copyright © 1982 by Thomas Nelson, Inc. Used by permission. The Holy Bible, New International Version®, NIV®. Copyright © 1973, 1978, 1984 by Biblica, Inc.™ Used by permission of Zondervan. All rights reserved worldwide. The Holy Bible, New Living Translation® (NLT). Copyright © 1996, 2004. Used by permission of Tyndale House Publishers, Inc., Wheaton, Illinois 60189. The Amplified® Bible (AMP), Copyright © 1954, 1958, 1962, 1964, 1965, 1987 by The Lockman Foundation. Used by permission. (www.Lockman. org). The New American Standard Bible® (NASB), Copyright © 1960, 1962, 1963, 1968, 1971, 1972, 1973, 1975, 1977, 1995 by The Lockman Foundation (www.Lockman.org). Used by permission.

Summerside Press is an inspirational publisher offering fresh, irresistible books to uplift the heart and engage the mind.

Printed in the USA.

"Every name Jesus bears
is an expression of
His person."

R. Lessin

Contents

Name
Above All Names

*God elevated him [Jesus] to the place of highest honor
and gave him the name above all other names.*

PHILIPPIANS 2:9 NLT

There is no one like Jesus! His name is above
all names. On His throne He reigns over all
creation—His kingdom above all kingdoms.
There is no other light we can look upon that will
outshine His glory.

In Jesus Christ we hear all that God has to say
to us. What God has planned for us and desires
to give to us is found in Christ alone. All our

hearts have ever needed or desired, the truth that we seek and the blessing we long for, is found in Him. There is no other person, no other source that God will use to meet our deepest needs.

Jesus is the Fountain that will quench our thirst, the Bread that nourishes our souls. As the Physician, He will heal our wounds, and as our Shepherd He guides our steps. Jesus is the Faithful One who can give our troubled hearts true security. As our Vine, He brings nourishment to our spirits; as our Door, He gives us access to the Father.

What love we have in Jesus! What a Savior for our souls, what a gift to our hearts!

May our hearts be open to receive Him, may our faith be ready to trust Him, and may our wills be surrendered to obey Him. As we commit our feet to follow Him, our hands to serve Him, and our actions and attitudes to honor Him, our lives become a reflection of His. May our voices magnify Him, both now and forever.

The True Light

The one who is the true light,
who gives light to everyone,
was coming into the world.

JOHN 1:9 NLT

No one has ever had his or her own star appear in the sky as a divine birth announcement. It is a truly unique occurrence, having a star appear as a travel guide giving directions to those who sought the place where the child lived.

One night, in one place, one special star appeared in the heavens for one ordained length of time, and with one specific purpose. The other stars in the night sky were lights declaring the glory of God, but the light of *this* star pointed the way to the one true Light. The other stars spoke of the great work of Creation, but *this* star proclaimed the coming of the Creator to earth; the other stars pointed to God's handiwork, but *this* star pointed to His mighty arm of salvation.

God still guides seeking hearts to the one true Light. As the world around us grows darker, the light of Jesus Christ shines even brighter. He is the Light of truth, of hope, of purity, and of beauty. That Light shines through the faces of those who know Him, through the eyes of those who see Him, through the character of those who walk with Him, and through the hearts of those who love Him.

A Son Given

Unto us a Son is given.

ISAIAH 9:6 NKJV

The most miraculous thing since creation happened when Jesus came to earth. When He entered the world as a baby, Jesus was God come in human form. He was Mary's baby, but He was God's Son. The Creator entered creation as a man.

Why did He do it? He came because His Father sent Him—not to impress us with His miracle powers so He could entertain us, not to educate us so we could learn more facts about heaven, not to provide us with new rituals so we could become more religious. Jesus came because we needed a Savior.

We had sinned and needed forgiveness. God wanted us brought back into a loving, holy, caring relationship with Himself. The only way we could ever be reconciled to God was by His Son coming and offering up His body as a sacrifice for our redemption.

What incredible love God has for you! Jesus came as a visible expression of that love...nothing is deeper than that love.

He came so you could have sweet communion with Him—a fellowship like no other. He came to be your companion always—a companion that is closer than a brother. He came so His presence could be within you—a heart-tangible presence. He came so you could be His holy possession—you can rest in the security of belonging to Him.

Lamb of God

Behold the Lamb of God!

JOHN 1:36 KJV

What greater witnesses could there be to the coming of the Lamb of God than those who tended their flocks by night.

The rich didn't witness His coming—they were too comfortable.

The powerful didn't witness His coming—they were too proud.

The religious leaders didn't witness His coming—they were too blind.

The merchants didn't witness His coming—they were too busy.

On a quiet hillside close to where Jesus was born, God made the news known. He spoke it in phrases of wonder, through creatures of splendor, to men of low degree. Those who were excluded from society's fancy gatherings would be included in heaven's greatest celebration. Those who had little education would come to know heaven's greatest revelation. Those who had few possessions would come to receive heaven's greatest gift.

Like the shepherds, God comes to us in our spiritual night to call us into His light. He comes in our spiritual poverty to call us to the riches in His Son. He comes in our spiritual loneliness to call us to the fellowship of His eternal celebration.

He who was wrapped in swaddling clothes has wrapped us in robes of righteousness. He has given us a mansion in heaven, the child who had no place to lay His head. The babe who cried as His mother held Him in her arms will wipe away all our tears.

The Word

The Word was made flesh, and dwelt among us.

JOHN 1:14 KJV

It has been said that the New Testament is in the Old Testament concealed, and that in the New Testament the Old Testament is revealed. In the Old we see the beginning of all things; in the New we see the end of all things. In the Old we see types and shadows; in the New we see substance and fulfillment. In the Old we see Mt. Sinai; in the New we see Mt. Calvary. In the Old we see the letter of the law; in the New we see the Spirit of grace.

The voice of the prophets speaks in the Old while in the New we hear the voice of the Son. Together, the books tell one story. It is the story of redemption revealed in time and space, through real people and actual events. It is His story—the story of the Redeemer and the redeemed.

Jesus established the law and fulfilled the Law. He is the message of prophecy and the fulfillment of prophecy, the promised sin bearer and the One who gave His life for our sins. In Jesus Christ the Old and New Testaments are like two musical movements that come together to make one glorious symphony, like the two lenses on a pair of binoculars that bring the image close and into focus, like the flames of two burning candles that come together to make one glorious light.

Provider

My God shall supply all your need according
to His riches in glory by Christ Jesus.

PHILIPPIANS 4:19 NKJV

From the beginning, it has been in the heart
of God to meet the needs of people. One of
God's names is "The Lord Provides." He provides
because He cares, because He loves, and because
He is faithful.

Redemption was God's plan to meet our
greatest needs—the need to be saved, to be
forgiven, to fulfill God's purpose for our lives,
and to be brought back into fellowship with

Him. God is also concerned about meeting our personal, physical, and practical needs as well as our spiritual needs.

When Jesus lived among us, He clearly taught and expressed what was in the heart of His Father. Jesus told us that when we see Him—His actions, His attitudes, His acts—we have seen the Father.

Jesus wants us to know that when we face a problem we don't need to reason it out—let Him work it out. He helps us to understand that there are no limits with God and no limitations to His power. Jesus works in ways that will build our faith, increase our trust, and strengthen our confidence in Him. He wants us to live a life free of worry and anxiety, fear and doubt, confusion and uncertainty. He wants us to be contented, totally resting within the arms of His loving care.

Intercessor
and High Priest

> Seeing then that we have a great High Priest who
> has passed through the heavens, Jesus the Son of God,
> let us hold fast our confession. For we do not have a High Priest
> who cannot sympathize with our weaknesses, but was in all
> points tempted as we are, yet without sin.
>
> HEBREWS 4:14–15 NKJV

Jesus lived prayer and taught prayer. He
prayed at different times and for various amounts
of time. He prayed in secret and He prayed in
public. He prayed about personal matters and

matters concerning others. He prayed for His friends and for His enemies. He prayed as a man dependent upon His Father, seeking to please Him and glorify Him in all things.

Through prayer He drew near to His Father so that He could draw us nearer to His heart. He knelt in humility so that He could raise us up to new heights. He poured out His soul so that He could comfort us in every sorrow. As our High Priest, He prayed for our unity, our sanctification, our joy, our love, our keeping, our ministry, and our future purpose.

Today, Jesus as your High Priest is praying for you. Think of it as you get up in the morning, as you go through your day, as you face your enemies, as you walk through your problems, as you return to your home, and as you rest in your bed—Jesus, the One who knows you best and loves you most, is praying for you.

Servant

*For you know the grace of our Lord Jesus Christ,
that though He was rich, yet for your sakes He became poor,
that you through His poverty might become rich.*

2 CORINTHIANS 8:9 NKJV

Imagine a large room filled with people. Each person in the room has great needs and is looking to the others to help fill those needs. Each person thinks *Here I am. I have arrived. I have many needs. I am expecting each of you to do your very best to make me happy, and if you want me to love you, you must give me a reason to love you.* That is how all of us have lived our lives. We did not live to serve, but to be served.

When Jesus came to us, He was like a man who entered a room full of needy people. However, Jesus said, "There you are. How may I serve you? You do not have to give Me a reason to love you, for I love you unconditionally. I hold nothing back from you. I give you My all, willingly, happily, freely."

The greatest change takes place within us when God's heart touches our hearts and we become extensions and expressions of His love to others. It is only from the heart of Jesus that we are able to esteem others better than ourselves, love others as ourselves, and honor others instead of ourselves.

Today it is Jesus' desire to put His love within your heart and cause you to ascend to the heights of His love by having you stoop to serve others for His sake.

Redeemer

Therefore My Father loves Me, because I lay down My life that I may take it again. No one takes it from Me, but I lay it down of Myself. I have power to lay it down, and I have power to take it again. This command I have received from My Father.

JOHN 10:17–18 NKJV

Who sent Jesus to the cross? Was it the Jewish leaders? Was it a mob? Was it the Roman government? None of these were powerful enough, influential enough, or persuasive enough to be able to do it. When He spoke to Pilate, Jesus reminded him that he had no power to crucify Him even though Pilate, as the Roman ruler, thought he did. When the disciples tried to keep Jesus from being arrested, He reminded them that if He wanted to escape the cross He could call a multitude of angels to come and rescue Him.

The One who sent Jesus to the cross was God the Father. The cross was the reason God sent His Son into the world. It was the will of Jesus to embrace the Father's will. Jesus said that it was for this reason that He came. It pleased the Father to bruise Him (Isaiah 53:10), and it brought joy to the Son to please the Father. It was in the heart of Jesus to redeem a people who would live for the glory of His Father.

His resurrection is our victory song, our shout of joy, our daily praise, and our eternal hope. Because He lives, we shall live also. He has promised it. He has guaranteed it. He has secured it. Jesus is our life, and heaven is our home.

Indescribable Gift

Thanks be to God for His indescribable gift!

2 Corinthians 9:15 NKJV

God's indescribable gift is not peace or joy, although His indescribable gift brings peace and joy. His gift is a person. His gift is Jesus Christ. When we have Jesus, we have everything.

All that our hearts have ever desired—every need we face, every truth we seek, and every blessing we long for—is found in Jesus Christ. There is no other person, no other relationship, no other provision, and no other source that God will use to meet our deepest needs.

His glory outshines the sun. No other counsel can replace His wisdom, and nothing overshadows His greatness. And yet Jesus gave Himself as a ransom for all. In Him we see all that God wants to reveal to us, we walk in all that God has prepared for us, we experience all that God has planned for us, we receive all that God desires to give to us.

What a love! What a Savior! What a gift! May our hearts be open to receive Him, may our faith be ready to trust Him, may our wills be surrendered to obey Him, may our feet and hands be committed to follow Him, may our faces be anointed to reflect Him, may our actions and attitudes be righteous to honor Him, and may our voices be uplifted to praise Him—now and forever.

Jesus

Behold, thou shalt conceive in thy womb,
and bring forth a son, and shalt call his name JESUS.

LUKE 1:31 KJV

When the angel Gabriel came to Mary to tell her the incredible news of the life that would be formed in her, the angel also gave her the name of the child. The name was not her choice, nor the choice of Joseph, to whom she was promised. The name was God's choice.

God chose a name that could, in one single word, put a spotlight on the reason why God's

Son left heaven and came to earth. They were not told to call Him "Wise" even though He was the Wisdom of God; they were not told to call Him "Creator" even though by Him all things were created; they were not told to call Him "Warrior" even though He is the Captain of the heavenly host.

The earthly name God chose for His Son was Jesus. In Hebrew His name is *Yeshua*. Yeshua is a name that means salvation. It also means a celebration of all that salvation brings to us. Even though Jesus could help people, heal people, guide people, encourage people, and bless people, it would mean nothing if He could not save people from their sins. Jesus means a celebration of victory over the greatest problem men and women face: the problem of sin. It is a problem that only God could solve, and it is a problem that God did solve through His Son.

Savior

We have seen and testify that the Father has sent the Son as Savior of the world.

1 JOHN 4:14 NKJV

*S*alvation means liberty from sin's bondage, forgiveness from sin's transgression, justification from sin's judgment, and life from sin's sentence of death. The celebration of salvation also means deliverance, aid, prosperity, health, help, and welfare.

In salvation we find everything that is good, but in sin we find everything that is bad.

Salvation represents everything that is right; sin stands for everything that is wrong. Deception and lies are at the heart of sin, while truth and verity belong to salvation.

Jesus was given the name Savior because He is the Savior. Salvation is not found in a ritual, a church, a creed, or in any good works that anyone can do no matter how sincere they may be. Salvation is in a person. God has only one Savior for the sinner and only one way to be saved. That way, that name, that person, is Jesus.

In the words of Bramwell Booth, "Yes, that is it! Christ the Savior! Not merely Christ the Helper of the poor, or the Feeder of the hungry, or the Father of the prodigals, or the Comfort of the sorrowful; but Christ the Savior from condemnation and guilt, from stains and filth, from the love and power and presence of sin."

The Christ

*And Jacob begat Joseph the husband of Mary, of whom
was born Jesus, who is called Christ.*

MATTHEW 1:16 KJV

The name Christ means Messiah. Messiah
means the Anointed One, the one sent by God
to be the Savior. For centuries the Jewish people
had known, through the promises God made to
Abraham, Moses, and David, that the Messiah
would come. The prophets also spoke of the
Messiah's coming. Isaiah proclaimed, "His name
shall be called Wonderful, Counsellor, The

mighty God, The everlasting Father, The Prince of Peace."

The name Jesus Christ means that He is the Savior of all who believe: the promised Messiah, and the anointed Redeemer of Israel. As God so faithfully promised, He is the light that would reveal God's heart for the Gentiles and the glory of His people Israel.

Jesus was sent by the God of Israel; He did not send Himself. Jesus was appointed by the God of Israel; He did not appoint Himself. Jesus was anointed by the God of Israel; He did not anoint Himself. No one had to tell Jesus why He was sent—He knew. He understood exactly why He had come. No explanation was needed. What's more, no motivation was needed as Jesus rejoiced in the plan to deliver mankind.

His place, His person, His position, His passion, His purpose, flowed out of the anointing He carried as Messiah, the one sent by God.

The Lord

They replied, "Believe in the Lord Jesus,
and you will be saved—you and your household."

ACTS 16:31 NIV

The name Lord is an awesome name. It is a
name that causes us to lift up our eyes and bend
our knees, to raise our hands and humble our
hearts, to celebrate with our voices and worship
in our spirits with reverential awe. Jesus Christ
is not just the Lord, but He is the Lord of lords.
He is the Master of all there is and the Ruler of all
that will be. He is in charge and He is in control.

34

There is no one in the heavens above or in the earth beneath who can be His equal.

When Jesus comes into a life as Lord, He doesn't come in to make suggestions, to plead His cause, to pamper and beg, to argue and debate, to manipulate and bargain, to push and persuade, to reason and debate, or to pamper and coddle; He comes into a life to take over.

When Saul met Jesus on the road to Damascus (Acts 9:1–9), Saul didn't get into a debate with Jesus or let Jesus know His point of view. Saul knew without a doubt that Jesus was His Lord. He immediately surrendered his life to Jesus' control and asked for his marching orders. "What would you have me to do?" was his immediate response to the voice of the One who met him and called out his name.

Immanuel, God With Us

"Behold, the virgin shall be with child, and bear a son,
and they shall call His name Immanuel,"
which is translated, "God with us."

MATTHEW 1:23 NKJV

*I*mmanuel means that God (deity) came to
be with us (humanity). God did not come to us
as an idea, a concept, a philosophy, or an ideal.
He didn't come as the sun, the moon, or a star.
He didn't come as a statue or an unapproachable
being. He came to us as a man. He took on

human flesh. Jesus Christ is completely God and completely man.

God with us—not in heaven, not out of touch or out of reach, not a phantom, not a shadow, not a legend or a myth, but God with us in grace, in truth, in mercy. God with us in human flesh—touchable, seeable, knowable. Love breathing, love giving, love caring, love dying. Walking where we walk, crying our tears, knowing our pain, feeling our grief, bearing our sorrows.

God with us—in the manger, in the temple, on the road, by the well, in the boat, upon the hillside, in the home, at the table; healing the sick, feeding the hungry, comforting those who mourn. God incarnate speaking to the multitude and seeking out the individual with arms extended, with words that beckon, with a voice that calls, "Come unto Me."

God with us—to seek, to worship, to love, to believe in, to follow, to proclaim, to cherish forever!

Wonderful

For unto us a child is born, unto us a son is given:
and the government shall be upon his shoulder:
and his name shall be called Wonderful.

Isaiah 9:6 KJV

Wonderful name He bears,
Wonderful crown He wears,
Wonderful blessings His triumphs afford.
Wonderful Calvary,
Wonderful grace for me,
Wonderful love of my wonderful Lord.

—Unknown

What Jesus does flows out of who He is.
He cannot deny Himself. Every name He bears

is an expression of His person. Because He is wonderful, wonderful things happen to those who put their trust in Him.

Jesus will keep everyone who trusts in Him at the edge of their seat, with mouths wide open in utter astonishment as He daily performs His wondrous works—wonders of mercy, grace, power, goodness, and love. His wonders cannot be duplicated because they go beyond man's capabilities, accomplishing what man is unable to accomplish, achieving what man is unable to achieve. Jesus Christ is wondrously, wonderfully, wonderful!

There is never a day so dreary,
There is never a night so long,
But the soul that is trusting in Jesus
Will somewhere find a song.
Wonderful, wonderful Jesus,
In the heart He implanteth a song;
A song of deliverance, of courage, of strength,
In the heart He implanteth a song.

—ANNA B. RUSSELL

Counselor

For unto us a child is born, unto us a son is given:
and the government shall be upon his shoulder:
and his name shall be called...Counselor.

ISAIAH 9:6 KJV

Isn't it good to know that Jesus is your Counselor? He is never too busy to see you. He is never late for an appointment. He is never in a rush to get you out of the office. You won't hear Him say, "You've come to the wrong place" or, "I cannot help you." Best of all, He doesn't charge by the hour!

What a joyous privilege we have to be able to freely go to the One who has all wisdom, knowledge, and understanding for the questions we have in life. He doesn't spend endless hours trying to figure you out and understand your problem. He knows your heart better than you do and knows exactly what you need. You can go to Jesus as your Counselor knowing that He will always guide you in the right direction because He will always speak the truth. He will always know what you need to do, and He will always be right.

His purpose is to show you the way that will please your Heavenly Father. He will counsel you to think as He thinks, to feel as He feels, to walk as He walks, to love as He loves, and to live as He lives.

Mighty God

For unto us a child is born, unto us a son is given:
and the government shall be upon his shoulder:
and his name shall be called...The mighty God.

ISAIAH 9:6 KJV

Jesus bears a name that only God can claim.
Humans and angels can have might, but only One
is the Almighty God. No person, angel, or any
created being can ever receive that name. They
have limits while He is without limitation; they
can only do so much while He can do all things.

Mighty God means that Jesus doesn't merely
sit in the number one place of power, but He

sits in the only place of ultimate power. Jesus is the Strong One. Jesus is the Conqueror who cannot be conquered. He is the Champion without a rival. He is not called "very mighty," "greatly mighty," or "mostly mighty." He is called Almighty.

Isn't it wonderful to know that you belong to a God who can't be pushed over, broken down, or beaten up? No one can stare down the Almighty or bully Him. The Almighty can't be debated, intimidated, or frustrated. The Almighty fears no one, is not threatened by anyone's plan, and is never forced to cancel any of His plans.

Jesus is mighty enough to keep anything or anyone from getting in the way of His will for you. No one has the power to stop His plan for your life. The world can't, people can't, circumstances can't, and the Devil can't. When He says yes to you, no one else can say no. No one can overrule Him, because He has the final say.

Everlasting Father

For unto us a child is born, unto us a son is given:
and the government shall be upon his shoulder:
and his name shall be called...The everlasting Father.

ISAIAH 9:6 KJV

*E*verything in Jesus and about Jesus is
everlasting. He is not a temporary Savior who
is filling in until someone else comes along.
Nothing about Him will go out of date or become
irrelevant. There will be no "new and improved"
updates to God's redemption plan.

In the world, things wear off, wear out, die out, or dry up. The fun or pleasure people experience at a party soon leaves them, and so they seek out a new party or experience that will bring them some measure of momentary satisfaction. But the reality of Jesus Christ in our hearts never becomes stale, empty, or meaningless. Jesus is everlasting joy, not momentary happiness. He is your joy today, and He will be your joy tomorrow.

All that Jesus was to you yesterday, He is today; all that He is to you today, He will always be, and more so as time goes by. Draw close to Him, and you will see more of His beauty; listen carefully to His voice, and you will hear Him speak new and glorious things; break bread with Him, and your heart will feast on His bounty; follow His footsteps, and He will lead you into the things that will last forever.

The Prince of Peace

*Do not be anxious about anything, but in everything, by prayer
and petition, with thanksgiving, present your requests to God.
And the peace of God, which transcends all understanding,
will guard your hearts and your minds in Christ Jesus.*

PHILIPPIANS 4:6–7 NIV

Knowing His peace, and having His peace
rule in your heart day by day, is one of the
greatest gifts Jesus can give to you. Peace is not
the absence of conflict but the presence of Jesus.
The peace that He gives to you is not dependent
upon the circumstances in your day but upon

your relationship with Him. The peace Jesus gives doesn't have its source in what is going on around you but comes as a result of His life in you.

Jesus did not come into your heart to bring you worry, anxiety, or restlessness. He came to give you rest. His peace will guard your thoughts from worry and keep your heart from fear. Because of His peace, you can be in harmony with God's will and purpose for your life. Through His peace you can know victory over every enemy that would try to trouble you. You can have the greatest measure of contentment and the deepest level of inward rest because of His peace.

Drop Thy still dews of quietness till all our
    striving cease;
Take from our souls the strain and stress,
And let our ordered lives confess
The beauty of Thy Peace.

—John Greenleaf Whittier

Man of Sorrows

He is despised and rejected of men; a man of sorrows, and acquainted with grief: and we hid as it were our faces from him; he was despised, and we esteemed him not.

ISAIAH 53:3 KJV

Jesus sought the lowly place so He could lift you up. He was rejected so you could be accepted. He was acquainted with grief so you could be comforted. His heart was broken so yours could be healed.

One of the ways that we see the heart of Jesus is through His meekness. Meekness is not weakness. His meekness means that He was totally submitted to the will of the Father. He who is Almighty and could have called an army of angels to rescue Him chose instead to learn obedience through the things He suffered. Meekness is heard in the prayer that Jesus prayed, "Not My will, but Thine be done."

We can see Jesus' meekness in what He didn't do as well as in what He did do.

He didn't defend Himself;
He didn't exalt Himself;
He didn't revile others when He was reviled;
He didn't slander others when He was
    falsely accused;
He didn't turn His back away from those
    who beat him;
He didn't hide His face from those who
    spit upon Him;
He didn't descend from the cross when He
    was mocked, challenged, and ridiculed.

The meekness, the sorrow, and the suffering of Jesus mean that you never need to question His love for you.

The Advocate

*My little children, I am writing these things to you
so that you may not sin. And if anyone sins, we have an Advocate
with the Father, Jesus Christ the righteous.*

1 JOHN 2:1 NASB

As your Advocate, Jesus is the one who pleads
your case. He is your comforter in heaven,
just as the Holy Spirit is your comforter on
earth. He who knows your sins is also the one
who has identified Himself with your sins. His
voice pleads on your behalf as your Righteous
Redeemer. Because Jesus is for you, it means that

nothing and no one can be against you. Because He is your defender, you do not need to try to defend yourself.

Satan's accusations against you are many. Jesus does not plead your innocence, but as your Advocate, He presents irrefutable evidence of the atonement that He has made on your behalf. As someone once said, "When you ask Jesus to represent you as your heavenly lawyer, remember that He has never lost a case."

Before a trial, a defendant is asked to plead one of two ways: "guilty" or "not guilty." For those who are in Christ, there is another plea that can be made, "I plead the blood of Jesus Christ on my behalf." You can rest your case in His hands. It is because of His shed blood that you are forgiven, cleansed, redeemed, and justified. You no longer need to live under condemnation or fear.

The Alpha and Omega

I am Alpha and Omega, the beginning and the ending,
saith the Lord, which is, and which was,
and which is to come, the Almighty.

REVELATION 1:8 KJV

Jesus Christ is the eternal God. He existed
before all things and He created all things.
He is the "Alpha." Jesus will always be, even
beyond time, and He brings all things to their
determined end. He is the "Omega." What began
with His word will end at His feet.

Jesus is the first and last—
He has the first and last word in our decisions;
He has the final say in every conversation.
His direction is the beginning point of our journey;
His destination is the place we want to arrive.

He holds first place in our hearts.
He is our first priority and final authority;
He is our first and only option.
He starts and ends things in our lives;
He sustains us and brings things to completion.

He is the sunrise of our morning;
He is the sunset of our day.
His mercy greets us when we wake;
His goodness covers us in the night.

The Bread of Life

I am the bread of life.

JOHN 6:48 NIV

"Bread" is another name for the provision God has given us to fully satisfy our spiritual hunger. Spiritual hunger is a good thing, but our spirits must feed upon the right diet, the true Bread that comes from heaven. In Isaiah 55 we read that God invites us to come to Him and feast upon His perfect provision. He tells us that His bread is available to us without money and without price, and we can freely receive all He desires to give. God's bread, God's provision, God's fullness is found in Jesus Christ.

Our spiritual daily Bread is made to be eaten, not to be set on a shelf and admired. Jesus is the spiritual Bread we eat. He is fresh, never stale, never dry, never void of nutrients. He is the perfect food, fully satisfying our every need.

All who are spiritually hungry have been called to partake of the life of Jesus by faith. Jesus is God's manna to us. Like manna—the daily food God provided to the Israelites while they wandered in the wilderness—coming down from heaven, so Jesus comes to us from the Father. We don't need to store Him away and save Him for another day. He is ours every morning and He will sustain us throughout the day.

Guide me, O Thou great Jehovah,
Pilgrim through this barren land;
I am weak, but Thou art mighty;
Hold me with Thy powerful hand.
Bread of heaven, Bread of heaven,
Feed me till I want no more,
Feed me till I want no more.

—WILLIAM WILLIAMS

The Beloved

For he received from God the Father honour and glory,
when there came such a voice to him from the excellent glory,
This is my beloved Son, in whom I am well pleased.

2 PETER 1:17 KJV

Jesus is the Father's Beloved. God spoke that name over Him when John baptized Jesus. God also spoke that name over Him when Jesus was on the Mount of Transfiguration. Each time the name Beloved was spoken, it was followed by the words, "in whom I am well pleased."

Jesus wants us to trust Him to live His life in us. He wants to share the riches of His life with us. The life Jesus lives in us is a life that will always be pleasing to the Father. It is a life of love—knowing God's love and showing God's love.

His Righteousness is the character of love;
His Holiness is the beauty of love;
His Omnipotence is the power of love;
His Omnipresence is the nearness of love;
His Omniscience is the mind of love;
His Judgment is the protection of love;
His Grace is the favor of love;
His Goodness is the practice of love;
His Kindness is the attitude of love;
His Care is the tenderness of love;
His Majesty is the glory of love;
His Giving is the expression of love.
His Peace is the rest of love;
His Joy is the celebration of love.

Jesus Christ, the Beloved, is the fullest expression of the love of God. He is love *incarnate*.

The Shepherd and Bishop

For ye were as sheep going astray; but are now returned unto the
Shepherd and Bishop of your souls.

1 PETER 2:25 KJV

*S*heep need a shepherd because sheep
need constant care. Sheep can't live in the wild;
they would never survive. Wolves have no fear of
sheep; it is only the Shepherd who can protect
against them. "For thus saith the Lord GOD;
Behold, I, even I, will both search my sheep, and
seek them out" (Ezekiel 34:11 KJV). In the same
way that a shepherd provides watchful care over

sheep, a bishop is a caregiver providing watchful care over God's people.

Sometimes, people who don't know us very well will say, "I am looking out for you." That comment sounds sincere, but it doesn't bring us a great deal of comfort. How can we have confidence that someone is looking out for us if they don't know us?

Jesus is not only the Shepherd who finds the lost sheep, but He is also the Bishop, the overseer. He knows and intimately cares for everyone who comes to Him. He watches over your soul, not just your physical needs. He cares about your well-being, your wholeness, and your wellness. He has joyfully taken the responsibility to look after you and tend your soul.

We are Thine; do Thou befriend us,
Be the guardian of our way;
Keep Thy flock, from sin defend us,
Seek us if we go astray;

—DOROTHY A. THRUPP

The Arm of the Lord

*The LORD hath made bare his holy arm
in the eyes of all the nations; and all the ends
of the earth shall see the salvation of our God.*

ISAIAH 52:10 KJV

The Arm of the Lord is such an awesome
name. Through this name God is telling us that
His Son is the extension of His might and the
expression of His heart.

As a young boy, I was in awe of the size of
my grandfather's muscles and the strength of his
powerful arms. Many times he would flex his

right arm and let me wrap my hands around it. When I did, he would demonstrate his strength by lifting me off the ground. I never failed to be in wonder of it all.

The Arm of the Lord reminds us of His tender care. It is His strong arm that can lift us, hold us, and keep us close to His heart. His arm has the power to anoint the eyes of a blind man and restore His sight; His arm has the tenderness to embrace a little child and draw him to His side. His arm holds the rod and the staff that give us comfort.

His arm also speaks of His mighty work of redemption when He died on the cross. The arm of the Lord is extended, not to forbid you access to His grace, but to pour His grace upon you in abundance. It is His arm of salvation that pulls you out of the miry clay and lifts you out of the horrible pit of sin and rebellion. The might of all other arms will fail to save. It is His arm alone that can rescue you.

The Foundation

*Therefore thus saith the Lord GOD, Behold, I lay in Zion for
a foundation a stone, a tried stone, a precious corner stone,
a sure foundation: he that believeth shall not make haste.*

ISAIAH 28:16 KJV

We cannot put our trust in people, in things, or
in the systems of this world. The world's greatest
kingdoms have fallen; the world's biggest armies
have known defeat; the world's noblest kings have
lost their power; the world's mightiest warriors
have lost their strength. Everything in the world
will suffer decay; everything is temporary. There
is nothing that is safe or secure that is based upon

man or his ways, and lives that are built upon poor foundations will collapse in the storms of life. Jesus, our Foundation, is the only one we can build our lives upon and not face ruin.

The Bible tells us that God will shake everything that is shakable; only what cannot be shaken will remain. Jesus Christ is the solid foundation of our faith. Nothing you have in Christ can be lost or destroyed when you stand upon His solid ground.

Let your life stand on Christ, for His foundation is unshakable.

Let your hope rest in Christ, for His foundation is unmovable.

Let your heart trust in Christ, for His foundation is indestructible.

My hope is built on nothing less
Than Jesus blood and righteousness...
On Christ the solid Rock I stand
All other ground is sinking sand.

—EDWARD MOTE

Our Passover

Christ our passover is sacrificed for us.

1 CORINTHIANS 5:7 KJV

"Christ our Passover" is a powerful truth. It tells us that what God did for Israel when the blood of the slain lamb was applied to the doorposts of their homes, God will do for us when we, by faith, apply the blood of the Lamb of God to the doorposts of our hearts. The result was that Israel was saved from the wrath of God that fell upon Egypt in the judgment of death (Exodus 12). Jesus our Passover means that in Him we will be saved from the coming wrath of God and His final judgment. Our deliverance from God's wrath is a real thing. If God's deliverance is real, God's judgment is also real. We can thank God every day that He has extended His mercy to us, that the blood of His Son, our Passover, has been slain for us and that we have passed from death unto life.

When Jesus Christ came to earth, He kept the Passover every year. At the Last Supper, He didn't just take the bread; He was the bread, broken for us. When He took the wine, He told us it was His blood, shed for the forgiveness of our sins.

Today, every believer in Christ who partakes of communion celebrates God's everlasting feast of Passover. We will continue to do so until we celebrate it with Him, our Passover, in His kingdom.

The Treasure

For it is the God who commanded light to shine out
of darkness, who has shone in our hearts to give the light
of the knowledge of the glory of God in the face of Jesus Christ.
But we have this treasure in earthen vessels.

2 CORINTHIANS 4:6–8 NKJV

*P*eople often ask the question, "What's life all
about?" Thankfully, God had the answer to that
question long before anyone asked it.

What's life all about? It's about the Treasure,
not the vessel; it's about His glory, not our
appearance; it's about His love, not our niceness.

Life is all about His purpose, not our plans; it's about His kingdom, not our agenda; it's about His reign, not our rights. It's not about our opinions, it's about His truth; it's not about our way, it's about His will; it's not about our efforts; it's about His life. To put it simply, it's all about Jesus.

Jesus Christ is God's treasure. He is more brilliant than any diamond, worth more than any jewel, more precious than any metal, more beautiful than any polished stone. His value will never diminish and His glory will never tarnish. His kingdom will never be conquered and His throne will never be overthrown.

To find Him is to find life's greatest treasure—He is everything good, true, glorious, right. Everything your heart could ever hope for. To possess all and not have Him is to be empty; to forsake all and have Him is to be fulfilled.

The Seed

What, then, was the purpose of the law? It was
added because of transgressions until the Seed
to whom the promise referred had come.

GALATIANS 3:19 NIV

$\mathcal{S}$eed always produces the exact life that is inside
it. It never fails. A corn seed will never grow
into a peach tree, and an avocado seed will never
produce a palm tree. As the Seed, Jesus is planted
in your life. The produce of that Seed is not the
life of your flesh or the life of the enemy. As the
Seed grows, the life of Jesus will be expressed

through you to others. You will think as He thinks—you will have the mind of Christ (1 Corinthians 2:16); you will live as He lives— you will have the life of Christ (Galatians 2:20); you will love as He loves—you have the love of Christ (2 Corinthians 5:14).

If we are having problems in our spiritual growth, the problem is not with the Seed. We must guard the life of the Seed and keep everything out of our lives that would hinder its growth and its fruit.

From the parable of the farmer sowing the seed we learn that unmanaged or neglected soil keeps the plant from taking root. The seed is snatched away or withers and dies. But, "the seed that fell on good soil represents those who truly hear and understand God's word and produce a harvest of thirty, sixty, or even a hundred times as much as had been planted!" (Matthew 13:23 NLT).

Light of the World

Then Jesus spoke to them again, saying,
"I am the light of the world. He who follows Me
shall not walk in darkness, but have the light of life."

JOHN 8:12 NKJV

The world is a dark place. There are many false lights that beckon us: *Look to me. Follow me.* If we attempt to walk by "false lights" (2 Corinthians 11:14), we only go deeper into darkness. But there is a Light that shines brighter than any lighthouse and can save any battered vessel from being smashed against the rocks of sin. Jesus, the Light of the World, will always banish the darkness of selfishness, evil, fear, confusion, bondage, and dead religion.

When Moses built the Temple, he followed God's pattern. There was an outer court which had the natural light of the sun; there was the inner court which had the light of the menorah; there was the holy of holies which had the light of the glory of God. The glory of God was the light of His presence.

The light that Jesus brings to us can only come from His presence within us. Jesus said that His light is the light of life. He lights up the deepest place within us—where we live, move, and have our being. When His light is in us we are spiritually alive. His light in us means that every step we take is a step of life. Following His light doesn't rob us, it restores us; it doesn't sadden us, it gladdens us; it doesn't weaken us, it strengthens us.

Amen

These are the words of the Amen.

REVELATION 3:14 NIV

When we hear the word *amen*, we often think of it as the end to a prayer. We wait to hear it as a clue that the person who is praying has finished. When Jesus says He is the Amen it means something far greater. It means that we can be certain about everything He is and everything He has to say. Think of it as God saying, "My Son has My final approval over everything He has said and over everything He has done."

When Jesus says amen to His Father's words, He is saying that He is the fulfillment of everything God has said. In modern language, saying "you can count on it" is a way of convincing someone that what we have said is reliable, dependable, and trustworthy. Amen is that and more. Amen is the vow, the guarantee, and the oath of God stating that everything He has said has been sealed with a binding promise.

Amen can also mean *verily*. When Jesus used it at the beginning of a sentence he was saying to those around Him, "Listen, what you are about to hear is absolutely true and accurate. Everything I have to say is exactly what you need to hear." Have you read something today in Scripture where Jesus has said to you, "You can count on it"? That is an Amen!

Life

*Jesus said to him, "I am the way, the truth, and the life.
No one comes to the Father except through Me."*

JOHN 14:6 NKJV

The following quote is something everyone
can relate to: "I had planned a great day for
myself, filled with the things I like to do, but
when I got out of bed, life happened and my
plans changed." Every day, for each of us, life
happens—people oversleep, burn the toast, hurt
their backs, get emergency phone calls, have
flat tires, lose their keys, miss a flight, catch a

cold, or experience a thousand-and-one other unexpected things. When we say "life happens," what we really mean is "circumstances happen."

Life as viewed through our circumstances is only one type of reality. A mother may say, "My reality is taking care of the kids." A business man may say, "My reality is meeting deadlines." Everyday is filled with the reality of the circumstances of life.

However, Jesus said that He is the Life—the Reality. Circumstances happen around us; the life of Jesus happens within us. The reality of Jesus Christ is greater than the reality of our circumstances. It is Jesus' reality ruling in our hearts. Life happens to everyone, but it is His reality that can keep us moving through our circumstances in quietness, in confidence, in righteousness, in peace, in strength, and in joy. When life happens, let Jesus happen in you.

Apostle

Wherefore...partakers of the heavenly calling, consider the Apostle and High Priest of our profession, Christ Jesus.

HEBREWS 3:1 KJV

*O*ne of the meanings of an apostle is someone who is sent from one place to another as an ambassador. An ambassador is an official representative of the highest rank. Jesus Christ is our Apostle, our "Sent One." He was sent from heaven to earth as God's representative and ambassador. "I have never spoken on My own authority or of My own accord or as self-appointed, but the Father Who sent Me has Himself given Me orders [concerning] what to say and what to tell" (John 12:49 AMP).

When people are in danger or trouble, a rescue team will be sent out to find those people and bring them back to safety. As a young boy living on the east coast, I went with my mother for a vacation at the beach. During our visit we were caught in a powerful hurricane. When my uncle learned of the danger we were in, he immediately came to rescue us.

God the Father sent His Son to rescue you. After His death and resurrection, Jesus told his disciples that He was sending them into the world in the same way the Father had sent Him (John 20:21). Jesus has called you to be His "sent one" and represent Him to the world as His ambassador.

Author and Finisher of our Faith

Looking unto Jesus the author and finisher of our faith.

HEBREWS 12:2 KJV

We have often heard the comment, "You can start well, but you must also finish well." This can leave us with a wrong impression if we take it to mean that Jesus starts our Christian life for us, but it's up to us to finish it.

We start out our Christian life by focusing our faith on the finished work of Christ upon the cross; we maintain the Christian life by focusing our faith upon the risen Christ; we carry a hope for our future by focusing our faith upon the second coming of Christ. Past, present, and future are all tied up in Christ alone.

We start well, live well, and finish well by keeping the eyes of our faith fixed upon Jesus, the Author and Finisher of our Faith. Jesus is the starting point and the ending point of our faith journey. You will finish well, not by seeing how many good things you can do, but by never taking your eyes off Jesus.

Looking to Jesus means to pay attention to Him and to put your focus upon His face. Looking to Jesus leads to following Jesus. What did Jesus do when you looked to Him for salvation? He saved you. What does Jesus do when you look to Him each day? He lives His life in you. What will Jesus do when you look to Him at the end of your journey? He will come for you.

The Bridegroom

He who has the bride is the bridegroom;
but the groomsman who stands by and listens to him
rejoices greatly and heartily on account of the bridegroom's voice.
This then is my pleasure and joy, and it is now complete.

JOHN 3:29 AMP

There are many things that can bring families and friends together, but a wedding is one of the most joyous. I recently attended the wedding of a member of our family. As we entered the church, we took aisle seats a few rows from the front. Soon the parents, grandparents, and special family members were ushered in and took their seats. Next, the groomsmen came out and walked the bridesmaids down the aisle. With excitement and expectation, everyone waited for the entrance of the bride.

The processional began, and the bride entered the back of the church. As the heads of everyone turned toward the bride, my attention shifted to the bridegroom. I intently watched him watching her. As she moved toward him, his eyes were fixed upon her. His face beamed with delight. He was overcome with her beauty. Tears began to pour down his cheeks. The closer she came, the more he glowed. He couldn't wait to make her his own. That moment helped me realize how much Jesus, our Bridegroom, is looking forward to the marriage supper of the Lamb and the coming of His bride, the church.

Bright and Morning Star

I am the Root and the Offspring of David,
the Bright and Morning Star.

REVELATION 22:16 NKJV

When in an airplane on a dark and cloudy day, it's always exciting to break through the clouds into the bright sunlight that shines above them. In the atmosphere of our lives, every moment that we soar above the clouds we experience the sunlight. Jesus is the sunlight in our day, and He is much more. As the Bright and Morning Star, He bathes the start of each day in brightness.

Sometimes when I get up in the morning, I sense that a spirit of darkness or heaviness has come upon me during the night. This sense of darkness, whatever the source, does not have to set the tone for my day. Jesus is my reality, and each morning He is my Bright and Morning Star. It is His light that sets the tone for my day, not my troubling dreams, not my feelings, not my temptations, not my subconscious mind, and not any spirit of darkness. The brightness of Jesus' name means that He makes the beginning of each day magnificently clear and good.

As the Bright and Morning Star, Jesus also brings hope into our day. We were made to hope, to plan, to imagine, and to anticipate certain things. We all need something to look forward to. Jesus is our hope and our expectation. He is coming one day according to His promise. He will not let us down. He will not disappoint us or fail to meet our expectations of a bright new day and a glorious forever.

Commander of
the Lord's Army

❦

*Joshua went up to him and asked, "Are you for us
or for our enemies?" "Neither," he replied,
"but as commander of the army of the LORD I have now come."*

JOSHUA 5:13–14 NIV

When he met the Lord, Joshua assumed He
was a common warrior, not the Divine Warrior.
Joshua was in for a huge surprise. He was not
confronting a human figure, but the pre-
incarnate Son of God. Joshua attempted to find

out which side this warrior was on and discovered that the Commander of the Lord's Army did not come to take sides but to take over.

Joshua did not meet a high ranking military officer but the commander and chief of heaven's army. He was in charge of the entire angelic host and His warriors could never be defeated. It didn't take Joshua long to discover that he was not on a battleground but on holy ground.

Jesus is your Mighty Warrior in every battle of life that you face. He has come to take over and be in charge of every circumstance you face. The next time you consider who is against you, quickly turn your attention to who is for you—the Father, the Son, the Holy Spirit, the heavenly host, the body of Christ, and the prayers of God's people are all on your side. You cannot lose, for He is victorious; you cannot be defeated, for He has conquered all; you cannot fail, for He will always lead you in triumph.

Captain of Salvation

*It was fitting for Him, for whom are all things and by whom
are all things, in bringing many sons to glory, to make the
captain of their salvation perfect through sufferings.*

HEBREWS 2:10 NKJV

It is dangerous to follow someone if they are
taking you in the wrong direction. The Bible calls
false leaders "the blind leading the blind." Many
people want to be leaders. Some take the lead
and others are appointed to leadership. Whether
self-appointed or man-appointed, every leader
should be asked, "Where are you going?"

The apostle Paul was a leader, but he didn't tell people to follow him just because he said so. He told others to follow him as he followed Christ. Paul said to follow his lead, but he never said that he was leading. Jesus was the one leading Paul, and Paul didn't want anyone who didn't want to be led by Jesus to follow him.

As Captain of our Salvation, Jesus leads the way to the eternal city and its glorious riches. Jesus is the pioneer, blazing the trail to heaven's door. He knows the way through the wilderness of sin, through the darkness of this world, through the traps and snares of the deceiver, through the quicksand of lies and deception, and through the labyrinth of false gods and empty worship. As a follower of Jesus Christ, you are a member of His holy band of brothers and sisters whom God is leading from glory to glory.

Anointed One

You know of Jesus of Nazareth, how God anointed Him with the Holy Spirit and with power.

ACTS 10:38 NASB

here is only one Anointed One, only one Messiah, only one Christ, only one Savior that God recognizes. All of these names are found in one person, the Lord Jesus Christ.

For many years, if a manufacturer wanted to make sure his product would be accepted by the public as legitimate, reliable, and dependable, he would hope to receive the Good Housekeeping Seal of Approval. God's Anointed One means that Jesus Christ has received God's divine seal of approval. God will never give that approval to anyone else. Every other god, ruler, religious leader, or self-anointed savior has been completely rejected by God. God's Anointed One means that you have found the only true One to believe in, to worship, and to follow.

Jesus Christ is not only the Anointed One, but He is also the one who was anointed by the Holy Spirit for the work God called Him to do. After His baptism in the Jordan River, Jesus went into the synagogue and read, "The Spirit of the LORD is upon Me, because He has anointed Me to preach the gospel to the poor; He has sent Me to heal the brokenhearted, to proclaim liberty to the captives and recovery of sight to the blind, to set at liberty those who are oppressed; to proclaim the acceptable year of the LORD" (Luke 4:18–19 NKJV).

Today, the Anointed One can anoint you with the Holy Spirit so that you can serve Him with power in a way that will glorify Him.

Carpenter

👑

Is not this the Carpenter, the son of Mary and the brother of James and Joses and Judas and Simon?

MARK 6:3 AMP

The name Carpenter tells us a lot about Jesus as a man, including His training, His skills, and His ability to work with wood. When I was a teenager, I loved the idea of working with wood and creating an object someone could use in a practical way. I took wood shop all three years in high school. Even though I loved building things, I always needed the help of my shop teacher. My biggest problem was lack of knowledge of the necessary steps needed to build something correctly.

When I finished high school, I was a long way from calling myself a skilled craftsman. A master craftsman is someone who works with excellence and clearly understands all the steps necessary to bring his work to its desired end. In a spiritual sense, we can also look at Jesus as a carpenter. He is the one who is building your life with the skill of a master craftsman. He knows where to cut, where to sand the rough spots, where to chisel, how to straighten crooked boards, how to apply the right amount of pressure to shape the wood, where to join things together, and how to apply a lasting finish. As He does His work within you, He does so with the finished work in view, and He knows exactly what He needs to do in order to bring that work to completion.

Chief (Precious) Cornerstone

Behold, I am laying in Zion a chosen (honored),
precious chief Cornerstone, and he who believes
in Him...shall never be disappointed or put to shame.

1 PETER 2:6 AMP

I joined the Army my first year out of high school. One of the first things I was taught as a soldier was how to march. It's not just walking. Marching meant walking with a group in an organized, orderly, and disciplined manner. Marching meant everyone went at the same pace and stayed in step, lined up with the person next to him. There was no room in the army for independent thinking or actions.

In order for us to march correctly, we were taught how to line up. We lined up in columns, and each column lined up according to the placement of the first man in the column—the anchor point. Before we could march, we had to be lined up with the point person.

The cornerstone lines up a building in the same way that a point person lines up a group of marching soldiers. It is the key foundation stone and it must be put in place first before any other stone is added. All other stones will be set in reference to the cornerstone.

Jesus Christ is the Cornerstone of your faith, your life, and your future. The only safe way to build your life is to line up each decision you make with your eyes fixed upon Jesus. Be sure that each step you take lines up with His perfect will for your life. That is the only way to live a fulfilling life.

Covenant of the People

I will appoint You as a covenant to the people,
as a light to the nations.

ISAIAH 42:6 NASB

The Scripture above is a powerful reminder
to us of who Jesus is and what He has done.
God's covenant promise was spoken to us in
His Word, but it was fulfilled in a person. Jesus
is our covenant! God's covenant promise to us
will never be invalid, because Jesus will never be
invalid. It is the perfect covenant, made by God
and agreed to by us.

Because Jesus is the Truth, the covenant is the truth; because Jesus is eternal, the covenant is eternal; because Jesus is trustworthy, the covenant is trustworthy. God will never break His covenant promise, because Jesus is the "Yes" of God to His covenant with us and His promises to us. Each morning you can arise and say, "The covenant of God is mine because Jesus is mine."

His covenant is a covenant of peace. It is a blood covenant sealed by the shed blood of Jesus Christ upon the cross. It is a covenant of grace and mercy. It is a covenant of salvation, of relationship and fellowship, of His life becoming your life as He works His will within you to do what is pleasing in His sight (Hebrews 13:20–21).

Dayspring

Through the tender mercy of our God,
With which the Dayspring from on high has visited us;
To give light to those who sit in darkness and
the shadow of death,
To guide our feet into the way of peace.

LUKE 1:78–79 NKJV

When we want to watch the setting sun, we look to the west. The setting sun reminds us that the day is over and the night has come. When we want to see the sunlight of a new day, we look to the east. The eastern sky reminds us that God is going to do a new thing. When the night sky is the darkest and the temperature is the coldest, that is when your hope can begin to soar. It is at that moment that the first light of a new day will appear before your eyes.

Are you going through a dark battle? Does it seem there is no hope in sight? Does it seem as though the dawning of victory's light will never come? Stand fast. Stand firm. Stand confident and full of hope. Keep your eyes on the Lord, and wait patiently for Him.

The Dayspring from on high will shine His glorious light over your situation. His light will not grow dim or turn away from you. His light will show you the next step to take. The way will become clear and the pathway of peace will open up before you.

Deliverer

And so all Israel will be saved, as it is written:
"The Deliverer will come out of Zion."

ROMANS 11:26 NKJV

As a kid during the 1940s, I loved going
to our local movie theater for the Saturday
afternoon matinees. Usually, there was a Western
movie to watch, a bunch of cartoons, and a
weekly serial. The hero in the serial always found
himself in great danger at the end of the episode.
By all appearances, it looked like he was a goner.
I would go home thinking, *There is no way he is going to*

get out of that one! It was always a relief to return the following Saturday and discover that my hero was rescued from the peril of the week before.

The apostle Paul could have been the hero in the Saturday serials of his time. Again and again, he found himself in hardships, in difficulties, and in great perils. Paul never would have been able to fulfill his calling and finish his course without the Deliverer to snatch him from danger and rescue him from evil. In his own words Paul tells us, "He rescued me from certain death. Yes, and the Lord will deliver me from every evil attack and will bring me safely into his heavenly Kingdom. All glory to God forever and ever! Amen" (2 Timothy 4:17-18 NLT).

Our walk with Jesus really is an adventure of faith. The Bible never promises that we will go through life without facing perils. The promise of the Lord to us is that He will be our deliverer whenever we face them.

The Door

Jesus said unto them again, "Most assuredly,
I say to you, I am the door of the sheep."

JOHN 10:7 NKJV

A popular TV game show would end its
program by presenting the winning contestant
with the option of opening one of three doors.
Behind each door was a prize, but only one door
held the grand prize. The drama of the show
was to discover what was behind the door the
contestant selected.

There are three doors that none of us should seek to open. Behind each one is something very undesirable. The first is the door of the world; behind this door everything is passing away. The second is the door of the flesh; behind this door everything leads to death. The third is the door of the enemy; behind this door everything brings darkness.

Jesus is the Door that will lead you to life and all that is good. The Bible tells us that every spiritual blessing we could ever desire or need is found in Jesus Christ—every treasure, every gift, every joy. When the door of God's mercy is opened to you, you can enter into God's abundance. It is here that you will always find the best. Through Jesus, nothing second-rate awaits you. Choosing Jesus as your Door will never leave you disappointed with the outcome. Opening His door means entering into life.

Faithful

Now I saw heaven opened, and behold, a white horse. And He who sat on him was called Faithful...and in righteousness He judges and makes war.

REVELATION 19:11 NKJV

*A*ll of us desire meaningful relationships where people can trust one another. One of the hardest things to overcome in any relationship is unfaithfulness. Once trust has been broken in a marriage, it is devastating and may take years to rebuild the damage that has been done. There are other situations where trust can be broken.

Someone may say, "I am having a hard time at work because I can't trust my boss." Someone else may say, "I trusted my friend with a deep secret, and I was shocked when he betrayed my confidence."

Trust is a word that is directly related to someone's character. We are not born with character. It is something that is developed in us. Trust is built in others not by those who are promise-breakers but by those who are promise-keepers. Trust creates security within a relationship.

Jesus carries the name Faithful because He is worthy of our complete trust and confidence. The Bible tells us that those who put their trust in the Lord will never be put to shame. He will never let us down. His words are true, and that makes Him believable; His actions are consistent, and that makes Him dependable; His power is limitless, and that makes Him reliable; His character is without flaw and that makes Him indescribable!

True

Now I saw heaven opened, and behold, a white horse.
And He who sat on him was called...True, and in
righteousness He judges and makes war.

REVELATION 19:11 NKJV

It is important for us to not only hear
meaningful things from other people but to
also know that people truly mean the things
they say. Scripture assures us that Jesus Christ
is completely true and sincere. His words are
not idealistic but realistic. He wants the words

that He speaks to us to lead us to faith, not to make-believe.

Jesus is true in His words; everything He said can be counted upon. Jesus is true in His motives; everything He does is for a right and good reason. There is no falsehood or deceit in Him. Jesus would never trick someone, con them into believing a lie, playact, or speak about fiction as though it were fact. Jesus is 100% genuine.

Jesus is true in His promises, true in His character, and true in His attitudes. He is true in His faithfulness, true in His kindness, and true in His love. His healing is true, His forgiveness is true, His mercy is true, His compassion is true. He is also true in all His judgments. No matter which way you observe Him, everything about Him is true and bears witness to the truth.

Firstborn from the Dead

*Jesus Christ, the faithful witness, the firstborn from the dead,
and the ruler over the kings of the earth.*

REVELATION 1:5 NKJV

When something is offered that you greatly
desire, you want to be the first in line to get it.
Recently, an electronic company came out with
a new game system. When the time of its public
release was announced, people stood in line for
hours in order to be one of the first ones to own
the system.

However, if there is something you are fearful about attempting, you are not as anxious to be the first one to do it. Two men were hiking in the mountains when the trail they were on led to the edge of a high cliff. In front of them stood a rickety, old wooden bridge suspended across a raging river hundreds of feet below. Without crossing the bridge, the two men could not continue their journey. They both agreed to continue, but neither wanted to test the bridge's safety by crossing first.

A group of Christians may all talk about the wonders of heaven, but most likely no one wants to go first. Jesus knows the fears that each of us has about death. As the Firstborn from the Dead, Jesus assures us that He not only tasted death for each of us, but He is also the first to rise from the dead, never to die again. Through our death, we will simply follow Him into our resurrection, never to die again. Jesus has gone first, and He is telling us that everything will be okay.

Forerunner

Where Jesus has entered in for us [in advance],
a Forerunner having become a High Priest forever
after the order (with the rank) of Melchizedek.

HEBREWS 6:20 AMP

When wagon trains crossed the country heading into the unknown territory of the American West, they hired scouts (forerunners) to go before the travelers to find out what was ahead and report back their findings. Pioneers needed to know where the trail would take them, if there were dangers ahead that they needed to prepare for, if there was fresh water nearby, and if there was a good place where they could make camp for the night. Most important of all, the job of the scout was to make sure the travelers took the best path possible, the path that would bring them safely to their final destination.

As Forerunner, Jesus is the one who has gone before us and blazed the trail to the Father's house. He has entered the sanctuary of heaven, into the very presence of God, and has reported back to us with all the information we need to arrive safely at our final destination. Jesus, our heavenly scout with perfect knowledge of what is ahead, gives us the basis to press on in our journey of faith with everlasting hope in our hearts.

Our Rest

But the Levitical priests…shall have linen turbans on their
heads and linen breeches upon their loins; they shall not gird
themselves with anything that causes [them to] sweat.

EZEKIEL 44:15, 18 AMP

$\mathcal{I}$n the Bible, a single word can be like a
powerful spotlight that reveals to our spiritual
eyes a truth of gigantic proportions. The word
sweat in this passage is one of those words.

Sweat represents the work, the labor, and the
natural efforts of our flesh. It was not the manner
in which the priests of the Lord were to minister

to Him in the inner court. The inner court was the place of God's presence, where the glory of the Lord rested upon the mercy seat.

Through the shed blood of Jesus Christ, the way into the presence of the Lord has now been opened to us. The work of redemption is Jesus' work alone. Our own efforts (sweat) can add nothing to His finished work. What is true of our redemption is also true of our ministry. Both begin at a place of rest.

The apostle Paul tells us, "I labored more abundantly than they all, yet not I, but the grace of God which was with me" (1 Corinthians 15:10 NKJV). Spiritual rest does not mean spiritual passivity. It is rest *in* action and not rest *from* action. God does not want us to serve Him out of the efforts of our flesh but in the power and strength of the Holy Spirit.

Our Hope

Paul, an apostle of Jesus Christ by the commandment of God our Saviour, and Lord Jesus Christ, which is our hope.

1 TIMOTHY 1:1 KJV

The Bible tells us plainly that the world is going in the wrong direction and moving there at a rapid pace. Today's political leaders make big promises but can only offer people a false hope.

God wants us to keep our hope in Him and not in this world's political system. Jesus has kept us in the world, but we are not of the world. He has us here for an eternal purpose—to be a light of hope that needs to be seen; to be a voice of truth that needs to be heard; to be a demonstration of love that needs to be lived.

Today we have a future hope. Our hope is not based on anything man can do or say, but is based on Jesus Christ—what He has said, what He has done, what He has yet to do. Our future is bright because His hope shines in our hearts. This hope is not fixed upon where the world is going but upon when Jesus is coming.

To keep our eyes on Jesus is to keep our eyes on hope. Hope is not wishful thinking but expectation of the promises He has given us and all the provisions He has made for us. Jesus will reign in righteousness, and there will be a new heaven and earth that is flooded by His glorious light. This is our true hope.

Priest

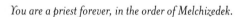

You are a priest forever, in the order of Melchizedek.

HEBREWS 7:17 NIV

Jesus' priesthood was of a different order and brought about different results than the priesthood of Aaron. The Levitical priests died and needed to be replaced; Jesus, our Priest, lives forever. The Levitical priests offered the blood of animals as an atonement for sin over and over again; Jesus, our Priest, offered His own blood as an atonement for our sin once and for all. The Levitical priests had to make an offering for their own sins; Jesus, our Priest, was without sin. The Levitical priests offered blood upon an earthly altar; Jesus, our Priest, offered His blood upon a heavenly altar. The Levitical priesthood was identified with the old covenant; Jesus, our Priest, is identified with the new covenant. The Levitical priesthood was imperfect; Jesus' priesthood was perfect.

You can be absolutely assured today that because Jesus is your Priest, He is able to save you. And He is, at this very moment, praying for you.

"Therefore he is able, once and forever, to save those who come to God through him. He lives forever to intercede with God on their behalf. He is the kind of high priest we need because he is holy and blameless, unstained by sin. He has been set apart from sinners and has been given the highest place of honor in heaven" (Hebrews 7:25–26 NLT).

Head of the Church

Christ is the Head of the church,
Himself the Savior of [His] body.

EPHESIANS 5:23 AMP

We were made not for a life of independent living but to be under the loving leadership of the One who made us. Isaiah reminds us that we have all gone astray and that each one of us has turned to his own way. Our own way always takes us in the wrong direction. We are sheep in need of a shepherd, we are ships in need of a captain, we are pilgrims in need of a guide. We cannot make it on our own. The good news is, God never intended us to.

When the Bible tells us that Jesus is the Head of the Church, it means that He is the head over a body of believers, not a church building. We are "living stones" that He fits together for His purposes. Individually and collectively, it is good for us to know Jesus is in charge—He has the right plan and is making the calls. He is taking the responsibility, for He is the most qualified. He makes the rules, and He has the power to carry things out.

Jesus, the Head of the Church, is the one who is in complete charge. We can be totally dependent upon Him.

Heir of All Things

In the last of these days He has spoken to us in [the person of a] Son, Whom He appointed Heir and lawful Owner of all things, also by and through Whom He created the worlds and the reaches of space and the ages of time [He made, produced, built, operated, and arranged them in order].

HEBREWS 1:2 AMP

When my dad was alive, for many years he would often start a letter to me with the following greeting: "To Roy, heir of the Lessin millions." It always made me smile when I read it, not because

I would be rich one day, but because I knew my dad didn't have any money. It is one thing to be called an heir; it is quite another thing to actually be the heir of something of great value.

God the Father has declared His Son to be the appointed heir, and that is no small thing. The inheritance is so great that instead of listing it item by item, the Bible simply sums it up by calling Jesus "The Heir of All Things."

It is even more amazing to realize that you, as God's child, are a joint-heir with Christ. That means that you share directly in the inheritance that is His. If God were to write you a personal letter today, it wouldn't surprise me if it began by saying, "To_____, joint-heir of My Son's millions."

Holy One

For You will not leave my soul in Sheol,
nor will You allow Your Holy One to see corruption.

PSALM 16:10 NKJV

During a cleaning project in our kitchen, I
decided the cabinets needed a fresh coat of paint.
All of our kitchen cabinets were painted white, so
I decided to check one of our closets to see if we
had any white paint in storage. I found a can of
white paint that had plenty left to do the job.

As I started the project, I soon discovered
that the white paint I was applying was not

matching the shade of white on our cabinets. I decided to go to the paint store to see if I could get a closer match to the white we had in the kitchen. When I got to the store I was surprised to discover how many different shades of white were available. Tints within the paint created a color range from off-white to snow-white and everything in between.

When the Bible tells us that Jesus is the Holy One, it means that He is "true whiteness" with all the tints (impurities) taken out. Every thing that we try to match up with the life, the character, and the nature of Jesus Christ turns out looking soiled and dirty by comparison. The way to be holy is not by trying to be better or live a cleaner, whiter life but by letting the Holy One live His life in us.

Sanctification

Of Him you are in Christ Jesus, who became for us
wisdom from God—and righteousness
and sanctification and redemption.

1 CORINTHIANS 1:30 NKJV

God is the one who sanctifies His people
through His Son, Jesus Christ. Sanctification
is not found in a set of rules but in a
person. Our sanctification is found in our
relationship with Jesus Christ.

If you were planning an elegant dinner,
you would not only take out the fine china

that had been set aside for such an occasion, but you would make sure it was clean before putting it in use. In the same way, sanctification has two main applications to our lives. One is that God sets us aside for His special use and purpose. The second is that God also cleanses those whom He sets aside. He wants your heart to be unmixed in its motives and pure in its devotion. The beautiful thing about sanctification is that you become conformed to the image of the One you serve.

As God's sanctified child, you have been set apart for something special in God's plan, not something ordinary in man's plan. God never wants you to think of yourself as insignificant or your purpose as being meaningless. He is your Sanctification, and you have been separated from the common crowd to be one of His holy people.

Good Shepherd

*I am the Good Shepherd; and I know and recognize
My own, and My own know and recognize Me.*

JOHN 10:14 AMP

*F*ew names have been more endearing to the
hearts of God's people than the name Shepherd.
It is the name that invokes thoughts of comfort,
tenderness, care, watchfulness, protection,
provision, guidance, safety, shelter, and security.
The name also creates strong emotion within us
because at its root it means "to keep company
with, as with a friend."

124

To shepherd is never part-time work. The Good Shepherd will never take His eye off you or leave you unattended. You are personally His and He is personally yours. He dries your tears and expels your fears; He cares for you more than anyone else and loves you more than anyone ever could. The Lord is the shepherd of your soul, the keeper of your life, and the guardian of your way.

"The LORD is my shepherd; I have all that I need. He lets me rest in green meadows; he leads me beside peaceful streams. He renews my strength. He guides me along right paths, bringing honor to his name. Even when I walk through the darkest valley, I will not be afraid, for you are close beside me. Your rod and your staff protect and comfort me. You prepare a feast for me in the presence of my enemies. You honor me by anointing my head with oil. My cup overflows with blessings. Surely your goodness and unfailing love will pursue me all the days of my life, and I will live in the house of the LORD forever" (Psalm 23 NLT).

I Am

Jesus replied, I assure you, most solemnly I tell you, before Abraham was born, I AM.

JOHN 8:58 AMP

*J*esus, the eternal I Am, is the I Am of everything you need, of all you desire, and of all you long to be. He is your wisdom, your authority, and your confidence; He is your purpose, your hope, and your future; He is your mission, your motivation, and your message. When Jesus says, "I Am" He is saying that He is all-in-all. He is your provider and your provision, whatever your need may be.

In trouble, He is your peace. In lack, He is your sufficiency. In changing circumstances, He is your contentment. In sorrow, He is your comfort. In hardships, He is your hope. In difficulty, He is your joy. In weakness, He is your strength. In battle, He is your victory. In impossibilities, He is your miracle worker.

He is your I Am when things are smooth and when things are rough, when there is sunshine and when there is rain. He is your I Am first thing in the morning, in the middle of the day, in the evening shadows, and when you go to bed at night. He is the I Am of every moment, of every ministry, of every appointment, and of every circumstance.

Unsearchable Riches

To me, who am less than the least of all the saints,
this grace was given, that I should preach among
the Gentiles the unsearchable riches of Christ.

EPHESIANS 3:8 NKJV

Do you know who you really are in Jesus
Christ? Have you discovered your true identity,
and are you living in the reality of it today? You
are the Lord's person and possession. He made
you and He owns you. He has ownership of you
through creation and redemption. Isn't it good to
know that you are doubly His? You are no small

thing to Him and your life is no small matter in His loving hands.

You are His, wholly and completely. There are no doubts in His mind or in heaven's records. The Devil has no lien against your life. Because of the purchase price that Jesus paid upon the cross, Satan has no rightful claim upon you. You are now God's child. You have been adopted into God's family. He is your Father and you are a joint-heir with Jesus Christ.

In Jesus Christ, there are no ties to your past to pull you back, no fears to hold you back, no chains to keep you back. The Son has set you free—you are a new creation, the old has passed away and the new has come.

Don't ever say, "Poor me." Instead say, "Rich me!" You have been lavished with riches—riches of grace, riches of mercy, riches of kindness, riches of faith, riches of love, riches of salvation, riches of glory, now and forever.

The Image of God

*God...has in these last days spoken to us by His Son,
whom He has appointed heir of all things,
through whom also He made the worlds; who being the
brightness of His glory and the express image of His person,
sat down at the right hand of the Majesty on high.*

HEBREWS 1:1–3 NKJV

Years ago there was a movie titled *The Invisible Man*. The main character lived and moved about like everyone else, but no one could see him. Even though this man had thoughts, feelings, desires, and a will, no image appeared in the mirror when he stood before it.

The Bible tells us that God is also a spirit and that no one has ever seen Him. Still, He is a person who thinks and feels. He has a personality, a nature, and a character. He is love, He is holy, He is good, He is faithful, and He is true. One of the many differences between God and the invisible man is that when God looks in the mirror, an image of His likeness does appear. It is Jesus Christ, an exact representation of who God is in His nature, His character, and His person.

We do not need a physical image of Jesus to know what God looks like. The Image of God is Jesus Christ, seen through the words He spoke, the works He performed, the attitudes He expressed, the mercy He extended, the love He demonstrated, the sacrifice He made, and the gifts He has given.

Because Jesus Christ is the express image of God's person we can gaze upon Him with the eyes of our faith; we can walk with Him in daily obedience, and we can talk with Him in constant communion.

Dwelling Place

*LORD, YOU have been our dwelling place
and our refuge in all generations.*

PSALM 90:1 AMP

One of the saddest stories in life is the plight of the homeless who live on city streets and parks throughout the country. These are people with a thousand different stories to tell but who all have one thing in common: the absence of a place they can call home.

Even more sad is the story of someone who is spiritually homeless. There is no greater emptiness, loneliness, or isolation than this. Jesus Christ came to make His home within our hearts. His presence makes it possible for every one of us to find our true and eternal home with Him.

The home that Jesus wants to establish within us is a home of splendor, beauty, and tenderness that will always make us feel welcome. A home of love where His arms are extended to help, support, encourage, and embrace. A home of acceptance where we are valued and celebrated; where He is genuinely happy to be in our company. A shelter, a refuge from life's storms. A place of fellowship where our hearts can open up in sweet communion with Him.

"In God the blessed man finds the love that welcomes. There is the sunny place. There care is loosed and toil forgotten. There is the joyous freedom, the happy calm, the rest, the renewing of our strength—at home with God."

—MARK GUY PEARSE

Tabernacle

And the Word (Christ) became flesh (human, incarnate) and
tabernacled (fixed His tent of flesh, lived awhile) among us;
and we [actually] saw His glory (His honor, His majesty),
such glory as an only begotten son receives from his father,
full of grace (favor, loving-kindness) and truth.

JOHN 1:14 AMP

The word *tabernacle* brings to us one of the
clearest revelations of the love and care of God
for His people. It says to us that God has chosen
to come to us in our need, to draw close in
intimacy and compassion, and to cover us with
His presence.

When God's people go through great hardships and heartaches we often wonder what can be said that will bring true comfort and hope. One thing we can say with strong affirmation is that God is there, in the midst of it all. This is at the heart of Jesus, our Tabernacle. Jesus didn't stay away from us, hiding from our sorrows in heaven. He came to us and tabernacled among us. In the midst of our deepest sorrows, tears, and struggles, God spreads the tent of His presence over us!

How close is God to us when we face our greatest trials and difficulties? The Bible tells us that God collects our tears in His bottle (Psalm 56:8) and that one day He will wipe away all tears from our eyes (Revelation 7:17). How close is God to you? No one can collect someone's tears in a bottle or wipe away someone's tears from their eyes while standing at a distance. To be a collector of tears means that God is not even an eyelash away.

King of Glory

Lift up your heads, O you gates! And be lift up, you everlasting doors! And the King of glory shall come in. Who is this King of glory? The LORD strong and mighty, the LORD mighty in battle.

PSALM 24:7–8 NKJV

Think of your life as a city that is surrounded by gates. The gates represent entryways into your heart, mind, emotions, thoughts, will, attitudes, motives, and spirit. Now think of Jesus as a conquering King who wants to enter the city of your life. He doesn't enter to occupy one or two areas of your life, but He comes to conquer the entire city—every low place, every high place, every secret place, every guarded place, and every busy place.

As the King of Glory, Jesus is strong and mighty in battle. However, His entry into your life is not a forced entry. He enters your gates as you throw open the doors. He manifests His strength and might not by knocking your gates down but by conquering every enemy that has laid siege to your life.

As your King of Glory, He comes to you with the brilliance of conquering love. He comes to free you from every battle the Enemy has waged against you, every lie that seeks to defeat and destroy you, every bondage that has robbed you of your joys, every sin that has darkened your soul, every stubbornness that has blinded your way, every stronghold that has oppressed your mind, every heaviness that has been a weight upon your heart. Lift high your gates, and let the King of Glory come in!

Rabbi

*Nathanael answered and said to Him, "Rabbi,
You are the Son of God! You are the King of Israel!"*

JOHN 1:49 NKJV

Not only is Jesus the King of all kings, the
Lord of all lords, the Master of all masters—He
is the Rabbi of all rabbis, the Teacher of all
teachers. We find His teaching to be very
different than that of most teachers we have
known. Jesus does not teach us so we can get
a good education, get good grades, establish a
career path, or get a good paying job. He teaches

us so our lives will be changed and will honor His Father.

Jesus' teaching points us to the facts and even more so to the teacher Himself. His teaching brings change to the heart not just knowledge to the mind. Our Rabbi does not want us to simply gain more knowledge, He wants us to know more about who He is so that we can be transformed into His image. As your Rabbi, Jesus is saying, "Know My words and learn of Me; learn of Me and you will become as I am."

The next time you study the Bible, hear a sermon, or attend a Bible class, keep this prayer on your lips: "Rabbi, Jesus, move what I hear from my mind to my heart, to my understanding, and to the way I live my life."

Physician

When the Pharisees saw it, they said to His disciples,
"Why does your Teacher eat with tax collectors and sinners?"
When Jesus heard that, He said to them, "Those who are well
have no need of a physician, but those who are sick."

MATTHEW 9:11-12 NKJV

Jesus is like no other physician you will ever
visit. As your Great Physician, Jesus examines
you and then prescribes Himself as the way to get
well. He is the best thing that could ever happen
to your body, your soul, your mind, and your
emotions. He can bring healing to every area of
your life that needs to be made whole.

As your Physician, Jesus has faced every form of heartache and human emotion. He was a man who was despised and knows how to heal the pain of disesteem. He was rejected and knows how to comfort those who have been ignored. He was a man of sorrows and knows how to lift your heavy burden.

Jesus experienced utter pain and knows how to touch every hurt within your heart. He was acquainted with grief and knows how to calm the storm of anxiety and calamity. He bore your sicknesses, distresses, and weaknesses, and knows how turn your ashes into beauty and your mourning into joy.

As you come to Jesus, your Great Physician, bring Him the burdens you carry, the pain you feel, or the hurts that have wounded you. Allow His healing balm to pour over you—to soothe, to calm, and to comfort. Receive from Him the tender ministry of His restoring hands.

All in All

Christis all, and in all.

COLOSSIANS 3:11 KJV

In baseball, if one team scores *all* the runs, the other team is shut out. If one candidate receives *all* the votes in an election, the other candidate loses by a landslide. If a doctor tells you to take *all* of your medicine, he wants nothing left over. The word *all* is another way God affirms to us who Jesus, His Son, truly is. If Jesus is the *all* of God, it means that God has eliminated every other option.

Although it has only three letters, the word *all* has huge implications. *All* means total, complete, or whole. Jesus Christ is God's All in All.

All things are reconciled by Jesus—"By Him to reconcile all things to Himself, by Him, whether things on earth or things in heaven, having made peace through the blood of His cross" (Colossians 1:20 NKJV). And all promises are fulfilled in Jesus—"For all of God's promises have been fulfilled in Christ with a resounding 'Yes!' And through Christ, our 'Amen' (which means 'Yes') ascends to God for his glory" (2 Corinthians 1:20 NLT).

All God's fullness, all God's treasures of wisdom and knowledge, all God's authority, all God's power, all God's blessings, all God's promises are yours today if you are in Christ. God has no other plan, no other purpose, no other provision, and no other person for you other than Jesus Christ.

God is calling your name.

Starting with a humble birth in a stable, God draws you to a place of worship, leads you to the quiet waters of salvation, shares the peace of His presence, reveals the simplicity of the cross, and offers the utterly amazing gift that only Love could give—His only begotten Son.

If you feel a longing to know more about God and eternal life through His Son, open you heart to Him through this prayer:

Jesus, thank You that You came to earth and died on a cross so that I can be forgiven. I admit that I am a sinner—I have done wrong and I need Your grace, mercy, and forgiveness. I turn from my sins and say "no" to a life of living for myself. I turn to You and say "yes" to Your will for my life. Thank You for being my Savior. I ask You now to forgive my sin. I receive You as my Lord and Savior. Thank you for giving me new life, eternal life. Amen.